DOMINOES

Lisa's Song

QUICK STARTER 250 HEADWORDS

Great Clarendon Street, Oxford, OX2 6DP, United Kingdom

Oxford University Press is a department of the University of Oxford. It furthers the University's objective of excellence in research, scholarship, and education by publishing worldwide. Oxford is a registered trade mark of Oxford University Press in the UK and in certain other countries

First published in Dominoes 2012

2016 2015 2014 2013 2012

10 9 8 7 6 5 4 3 2 1

ISBN: 978 0 19 424952 2 Book
ISBN: 978 0 19 424950 8 Book and MultiROM Pack

MultiROM not available separately

Printed in China

This book is printed on paper from certified and well-managed sources

ACKNOWLEDGEMENTS

Cover photograph by: Alamy Images (boy playing guitar/Elliot Elliot/Johner Images)

Illustrations by: Paule Trudel Bellemare\Lemonade Illustration

The publisher would like to thank the following for permission to reproduce photographs: Apple Inc pp.7 (iPhone 4s), 26 (iPhone 4s); Corbis pp.24 (Young Michael Jackson/Neal Preston), 25 (The Beatles/Bettmann); Oxford University Press p.30 (Wall/Corel)

DOMINOES

Series Editors: Bill Bowler and Sue Parminter

Lisa's Song

Lesley Thompson

To Nina

Illustrated by Paule Trudel Bellemare

Lesley Thompson was born in Newcastle-upon-Tyne, in the North of England, but she moved to Spain some years ago, and now lives near Alicante. She loves reading, the cinema, music, laughing with her friends, and looking at the sea. She also enjoys walking in the countryside in England and Spain, and one day she hopes to walk the Camino de Santiago in northern Spain. Lesley has also written *Deep Trouble*, *The Real McCoy & Other Ghost Stories*, and has adapted *The Secret Agent* in the Dominoes series.

Story Characters

Jack Brown

Alice Brown

Mr Brown

Mrs Brown

Al

Lisa

Emma

Ben

Mick

Contents

BEFORE READING

1 Write the family words in the correct places.

father grandfather little sister mother son

a Al is Mr and Mrs Brown's . . . .

b Jack is Al's . . . .

c Mr Brown is Al's . . . .

d Lisa is Al's . . . .

e Mrs Brown is Al's . . . .

2 Complete the sentences.

The oldest in the family tree is . . . .

The youngest in the family tree is . . . .

3 Match the words and pictures. Use a dictionary to help you.

a

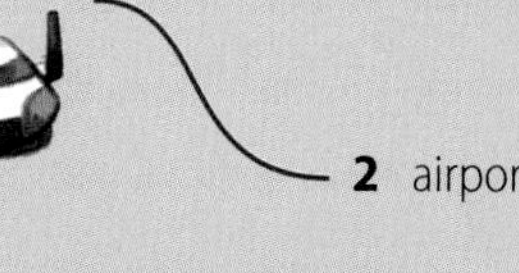

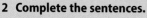

1 Internet café

d

2 airport

b

3 war

e

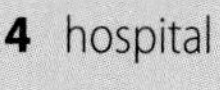

4 hospital

c

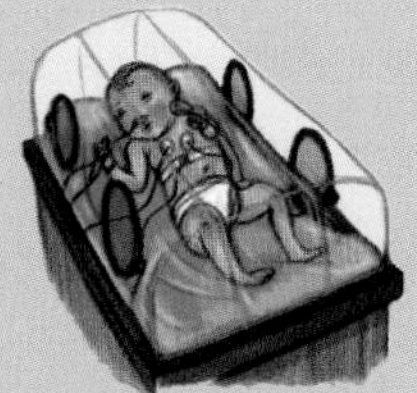

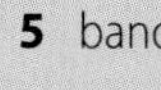

5 band

f

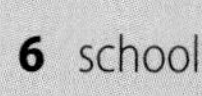

6 school

Chapter 1 Al's first love

Al Brown is thirteen. He lives with his **parents** in a little house. It's in Nottingham in England. The family are happy, but they have not got much money. So life is not easy.

When our story begins, Mrs Brown is **expecting** a **baby**. Al is waiting excitedly for his new little brother or sister.

parent a mother or father

life what you live

expecting waiting to have

baby a very young child

music people listen or dance to this

guitar you play music on this with your hands; it is made of wood with strings

band a number of people who all play music

drum you play music on this by hitting it with your hand or a stick

song music and words that you sing

Al's first love is **music**. He can play the **guitar** very well. He is in a **band,** *Fast Cars*, with three of his friends. They are Emma, Mick, and Ben. Ben and Al play the guitars in the band. Emma sings, and Mick plays the **drums**.

Al writes **songs** for the band. They play at Ben's house. Al's parents often come and listen to them. They are good friends with Ben's parents.

'Our boy can't live without his music,' Al's parents tell everyone.

ACTIVITIES

READING CHECK

Match the sentences with the pictures.

1

2

3

4

a He writes songs for the band *Fast Cars*. ....1.........

b *Fast Cars* play at his house. ....

c He plays the drums. ....

d She sings in the band. ....

e They play the guitars in the band. ...., ...

f She's the only girl in the band. ....

GUESS WHAT

What happens in the next chapter? Tick two boxes to finish each sentence.

a Mrs Brown …

1 ☐ has the baby.

2 ☐ goes to London.

3 ☐ needs to sleep.

b Al …

1 ☐ helps his parents in the house.

2 ☐ visits his grandfather.

3 ☐ writes new songs for the band.

Chapter 2 Al's baby sister

One morning, Mrs Brown does not feel well.

'The baby's coming,' she says.

'But it's six weeks early!' Mr Brown cries.

'Yes, I know. But please take me to the **hospital**. This baby can't wait!'

Mrs Brown is right. After six hours, Lisa arrives. She is beautiful, but she is very little. She must stay in hospital for two weeks.

When Lisa comes home, life is not the **same**. The baby cries a lot, and she doesn't eat much. Is the little girl all right?

Everyone is tired. When Al **tries** to play his guitar, his mother says, 'Ssssh! Lisa's sleeping!' Mr Brown says, 'You must help more in the house, Al. Your mother's very tired.'

Al tries to help but he is tired too. He can't **concentrate** at **school**, and he forgets to do his **homework**.

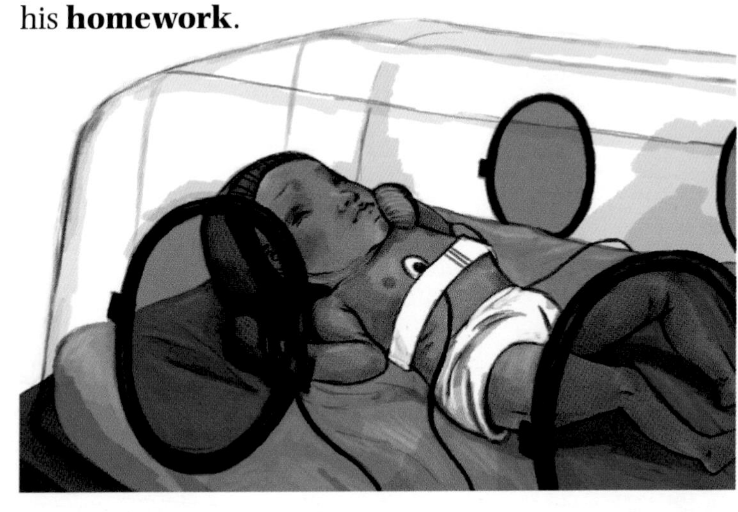

hospital you go to this building when you are ill

same not different

try to want to do something but not to do it well

concentrate to think carefully about only one thing

school students learn here

homework when you learn at home, usually in the evening or at the weekend

alone with nobody

short not long

One day, Al visits his grandfather, Jack Brown. The old man lives **alone**.

Al says, 'Mum and Dad never listen to me now. They're always with Lisa.'

'A new baby is a lot of work,' Jack says. 'You must understand that, Al. But what about you? Are you writing any new songs? You're a good song writer.'

Al says nothing to his grandfather. He has no time for the band these days.

When Jack is alone, he takes out an old photograph. He looks at it. It is a picture of his sister, Alice.

'Life's **short**, Al,' he says quietly. 'Be good to your sister. You're older. But you don't always know best.'

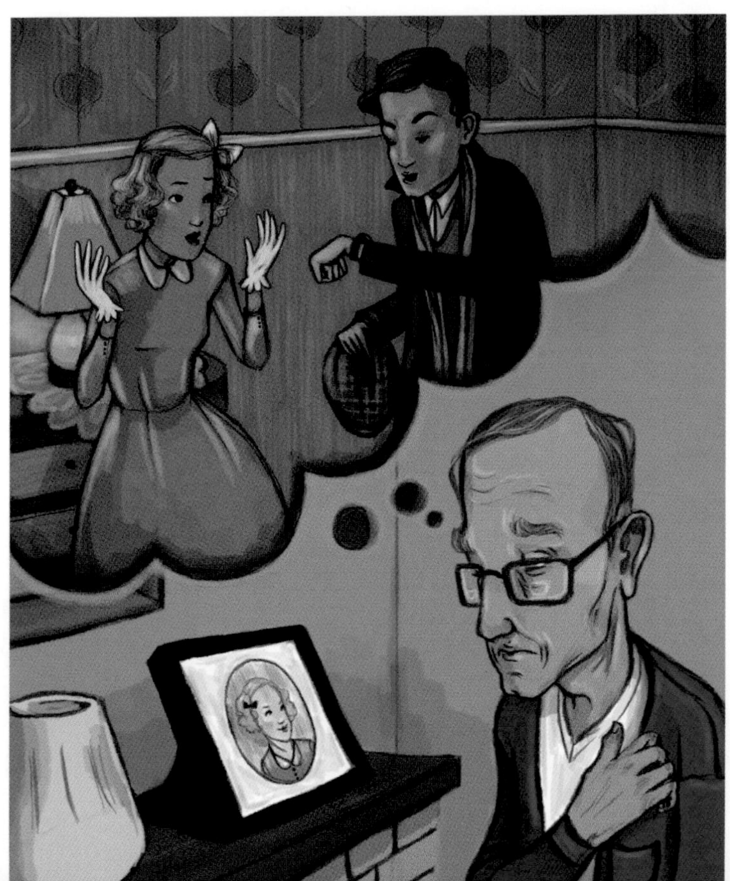

ACTIVITIES

READING CHECK

Are these sentences true or false? Tick the boxes.

	True	False
a Lisa arrives late.	☐	☑
b She is in hospital for two weeks.	☐	☐
c Everyone in Al's house is tired.	☐	☐
d Al does his homework every evening.	☐	☐
e Jack Brown goes and lives with his son.	☐	☐
f Jack asks Al about his songs.	☐	☐
g Jack looks at a photo of his brother.	☐	☐

GUESS WHAT

What happens in the next chapter? Circle the best words in the sentences.

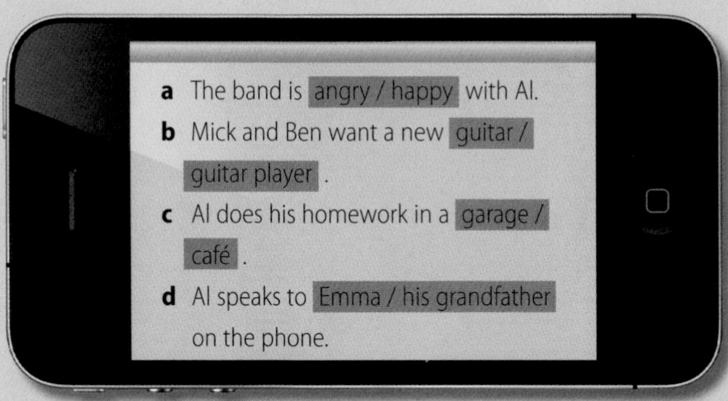

a The band is angry / happy with Al.

b Mick and Ben want a new guitar / guitar player.

c Al does his homework in a garage / café.

d Al speaks to Emma / his grandfather on the phone.

Chapter 3 Al's angry friends

Al's friends are waiting for him at Ben's house. Al is late again.

'Where is he?' Emma asks. 'We can't begin playing without him.'

'He's always late these days,' Ben says angrily. 'And he can't concentrate. Let's look for a different guitar player? My brother wants to be in the band.'

'You're right,' says Mick. 'Let's find someone new.'

Emma does not want to lose Al. She calls him on her **mobile phone**.

'Where are you? We're waiting for you. Get here fast, and say sorry. Then perhaps we can forget these last weeks. But you must change, Al. You must give more time to the band.'

mobile phone (**mobile** *for short*) a phone that you can carry with you

Al is in an **internet café**. He is trying to do his homework.

'Emma, things aren't easy for me these days. I can't work at home. Lisa's always crying, my parents are always with her. They tell me, "Do this! Do that!" Now you're doing the same. Leave me alone!' And he stops the call and puts the phone down.

Emma is very angry. 'I'm trying to help Al. But he's not interested,' she thinks. She quickly **sends** him a phone **message**: *Fast Cars is looking 4 a new guitar player. Don't* ***worry*** *about us. We don't need U any more, Al. GOODBYE!*

Al tries to phone Emma, but she doesn't answer. How does he feel? Bad. He does not want to lose his friends. And he loves playing in the band. But what can he do now? Just then, his phone **rings** again. This time it's his grandfather.

internet café you can have a drink or something to eat and can use computers here

send to make something go from one phone to a different phone

message you write this to someone; you say this into a phone for someone to listen to later

worry to be unhappy about something and to think about it all the time

ring to make a noise (of a telephone) when someone calls you

READING CHECK

Put these sentences in the correct order. Number them 1–6.

- **a** Emma phones Al. ☐
- **b** Al's Grandad phones him. ☐
- **c** Al phones Emma but she doesn't answer. ☐
- **d** Al stops Emma's phone call suddenly. ☐
- **e** Emma, Mick and Ben wait for Al. [1]
- **f** Emma sends a phone message to Al. ☐

GUESS WHAT

What happens in the next chapter? Tick two boxes to finish each sentence.

Mr Brown…

- **a** ☐ tells Al something important about Lisa.
- **b** ☐ buys a new car.
- **c** ☐ answers Al's different questions.

Jack Brown…

- **a** ☐ sends a phone message to Al.
- **b** ☐ tries to help his grandson.
- **c** ☐ gives some money to his family.

Chapter 4 Something is wrong

Al does not answer his mobile, and his grandfather does not leave a message for him. 'I can phone him later,' Al thinks.

When Al goes home, something is wrong. His mother's eyes are red, and his father's face is white.

'What's the matter?' Al asks.

'It's your sister,' Dad says. 'She's ill.'

'Ill?'

'Her **heart** isn't right, Al. She needs an **operation** and quickly.'

'Oh.'

'There's more. It's a **difficult** operation. No hospital in England can do it. Lisa needs to go to the United States for it.'

'I see. So when are you going?'

'We don't know. The operation's expensive. And there are the plane tickets and the hotel, too.' Mr Brown tries to smile. 'But we can find the money. Don't worry about it.'

Now Al is very **sad** and alone. Lisa is very ill, he knows. Perhaps he can phone Emma? Then, on his mobile, he sees a message from his grandfather:

Come and see me. I know about Lisa.

Jack is waiting for Al. He is thinking about his sister Alice, dead at thirteen. Suddenly Al runs in.

'Grandad, what can we do? Where can we find the money for Lisa's operation?'

'Take it easy, Al,' says Grandad. 'I've got an **idea**.

heart this is in you; it sends the blood round your body

operation when people do something to your body in hospital to make you well

difficult not easy

sad not happy

idea something that you think

Tell your friends in the band. Write a song for Lisa.'

'A song for Lisa? How can that help?'

'**Trust** me, Al. It can. Go home now and write your song.'

trust to believe that someone is nice and good

ACTIVITIES

READING CHECK

Choose the right words to finish the sentences.

1 Mrs Brown's eyes are red because …
- **a** she can't see Al. ☐
- **b** she is sad about Lisa. ☑
- **c** she doesn't like her family. ☐

2 Lisa must go to America because …
- **a** her brother lives there. ☐
- **b** she hasn't got any money. ☐
- **c** she needs an operation. ☐

3 Al is not happy because …
- **a** his sister is very ill. ☐
- **b** his grandfather lives far away. ☐
- **c** nobody likes him. ☐

4 Jack sends a phone message to Al because …
- **a** he can't speak. ☐
- **b** Emma is at his house. ☐
- **c** he wants to help his grandson. ☐

5 Alice can't help her brother because …
- **a** she is in America. ☐
- **b** she is dead now. ☐
- **c** she is angry with Jack. ☐

6 Jack tells Al, …
- **a** 'Write a song.' ☐
- **b** 'Go to America.' ☐
- **c** 'Say sorry to your friends.' ☐

GUESS WHAT

What happens in the next chapter? Tick the boxes.	**Yes**	**No**
a Al goes back to the band.	☐	☐
b Al writes a song about Lisa.	☐	☐
c Jack learns to play the guitar.	☐	☐
d Emma leaves the band.	☐	☐
e *Fast Cars* play for their friends and family.	☐	☐
f Al and his friends don't make any money.	☐	☐
g Al sings about Lisa.	☐	☐

Chapter 5 Back to the band

Back home, Al talks to his parents.

'I want to write a song for Lisa. I want to tell everyone about her.'

Mr and Mrs Brown smile. 'What a nice idea!' his mum says. 'Thanks, Al.'

Al phones his friends. He meets them at Ben's house. He says sorry. Then he tells them all about Lisa and the song. Emma looks at Mick and Ben.

'What do you think, boys? Can Al come back to the band now?' she asks.

'Yes,' Ben laughs. 'We need him. My brother can't play the guitar at all!'

'And he can't write songs!' Mick says.

'I've got an idea,' Emma says. 'We can play Al's new song at our **gig**.'

'What gig?' Al asks.

'The gig for Lisa!' Emma says. 'People can **pay** at the door. With their help, Lisa can have her operation.'

'Good idea!' Ben cries excitedly. 'Let's tell people about it on our **website**.'

So Mick puts the day and time of their next gig up on the band's website.

gig when people play pop or rock music for other people

pay to give money for something

website a place on the Internet where you can find information about people or things

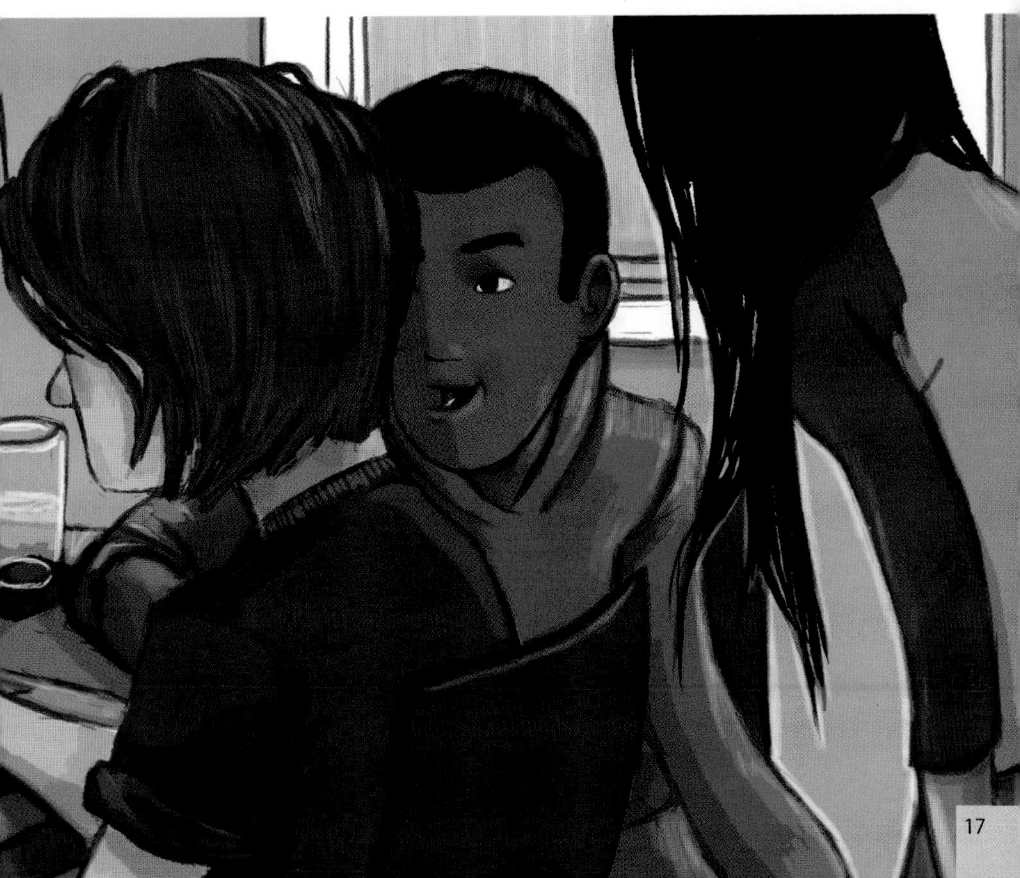

Two weeks later, after lots of work, the band plays at Al's school. Al's family and friends are there. Late in the evening, Al sings 'Lisa's Song'. Some people from the **radio** are there, too. They **record** the song.

Let's sing for Lisa and her life.
The **future**'s in her eyes of blue.
A **bright** tomorrow's in her smile.
So let's all help those times **come true**!

Next day, Al and his friends look at the money from the gig. How much is there? Can Lisa have her operation now?

radio you can listen to music and people talking on this

record to copy music and other sounds so that you can listen to them later

future the time that is coming

bright not dark

come true to begin to be true

READING CHECK

Use the words in the drums to write sentences about Chapter 5.

a Al's mother ......thanks her son for Lisa's Song...... .
b Emma, Mick and Ben ....
c Ben ....
d Al and his friends ....
e Al ....
f Some people ....
g Al and his friends ....

GUESS WHAT

What happens in the next chapter? Choose the best word.

a *Fast Cars* want to make more money / friends . ...
b People pay to write / hear *Lisa's Song*. ....
c Lisa goes to America / London . ...
d Jack and Al go to the hospital / airport . ...
e Jack remembers his young sister / daughter . ...
f Jack and Al go back home / to a gig . ...

Chapter 6 Past concerts, future gigs

'We need more money,' Al says.

'Then let's put *Lisa's Song* on our website!' Ben cries. 'People can pay for it and **download** it.'

People hear about *Lisa's Song* on the radio. They pay and download it from the website. Soon Al's family have the money for America.

—•—

download to copy something from a website to a computer

At the airport, Al and his grandfather say goodbye. 'Good luck!' Al calls to his parents and Lisa.

Suddenly Jack remembers a night in 1941. His mother is dead. His father is away at the **war**. He is the man of the house now. Night after night, planes **drop** their **bombs** on their town. People are afraid. His sister Alice wants to sing and **dance** and forget the war. He hears her words that night and his answer.

'Please can I go out, Jack? I want to sing at the **concert**. My friends are waiting.'

'No, Alice! You're thirteen! You must stay at home.'

Later, he is working at the hospital. Bombs are dropping. The sky is red. Then someone says, 'Jack, there's a bomb in your street. Your house is **on fire**!'

'Alice!' he cries. He runs home, but he can do nothing. He never sees Alice again.

war fighting between countries

drop to let something go down fast; to go down fast

bomb a thing which explodes noisily and can kill people and break buildings

dance to move your body and feet to music

concert when people play music and sing for other people to listen

on fire red, hot and burning

'What's the matter, Grandad?' Al asks. Jack smiles at his grandson. He sees a lot of Alice in the boy. Sometimes past **experience** teaches you things.

'Oh, it's not important now. But you must write some more songs. When's the band's next conce... er... gig?'

'Soon, Grandad.'

With that, grandfather and grandson leave the airport and go home.

experience when things happen to you

ACTIVITIES

READING CHECK

Choose the best answer.

1 Where do people hear about *Lisa's Song*?

1 At a new gig.	**2** On the radio.	**3** On TV.

2 Where can people buy *Lisa's Song*?

1 On the Internet.	**2** In a shop.	**3** At a gig.

3 Where does Al say goodbye to Lisa?

1 At the hospital.	**2** At home.	**3** At the airport.

4 What does Jack remember?

1 His first car.	**2** A day in the war.	**3** An old song.

5 Why does Alice die?

1 She is ill.	**2** A bus hits her.	**3** A bomb kills her.

6 What do Alice and Al love?

1 Dancing.	**2** Music.	**3** Writing.

WHAT NEXT?

What happens after the story ends? Complete these sentences with your ideas.

a Al and his friends . . . .

b Jack Brown . . . .

c Lisa . . . .

d Mr and Mrs Brown . . . .

Project A *A song review*

1 Read the song review and complete the information in the box.

Ben is a song from Michael Jackson's second album (1972) for the Motown record label. The name of the album is also Ben. The song is from a 1972 horror film. In the film, *Ben* is a killer rat and he meets a young boy, Danny Garrison. The song is about finding a friend.
The words of the song are by lyrics writer Don Black and the music is by Walter Scharf.
The song lasts 2 minutes 44 seconds. Jackson sings it with lots of feeling, and I like it very much. I give it four out of five.

Name of song: ......Ben................................
What's it about? ....
Name and date of album: ....
Name of record label: ....
Name of composer: ....
Name of lyrics writer: ..Don Black..................
Name of singer: ....
How long is it? ....
Personal star rating: ..Four out of five..........
Why: ....

PROJECTS

2 Read the information about a different song and complete the text.

Name of song: *Eleanor Rigby*
What's it about? Lonely people
Name and date of album: *Revolver*, 1966
Name of record label: Parlophone

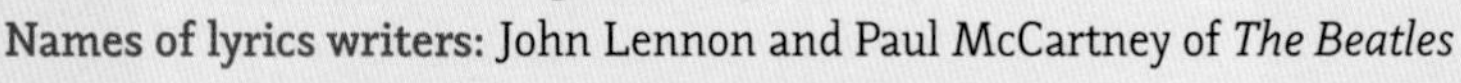

Names of lyrics writers: John Lennon and Paul McCartney of *The Beatles*
Names of composers: Lennon/McCartney, George Martin
How long is it? two minutes, six seconds

Personal star rating: Four and a half out of five. One of the most important pop songs. Sad but beautiful lyrics and music.

Eleanor Rigby is a song from *The* ....' seventh album (19...) for the .... record label. The name of the album is .... The song is about Eleanor Rigby and Father McKenzie – two .... The lyrics of the song are by .... and .... The music is by them and the Beatles' producer, ... The song lasts .... minutes and .... seconds. For me, it's one of the .... pop songs of all time and I give it .... The music and the .... are sad but beautiful.

3 Find a song with a person's name in the title. Make notes about it. Then write a review.

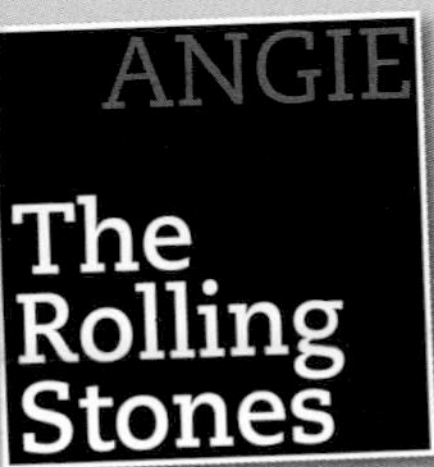

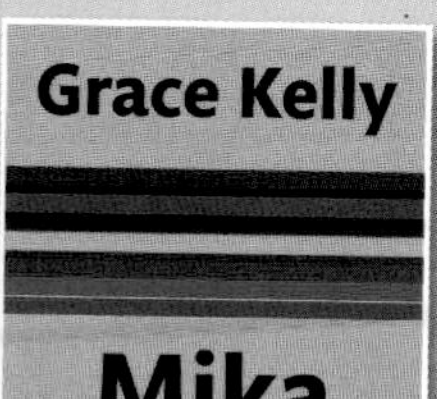

Project B *Writing a text message*

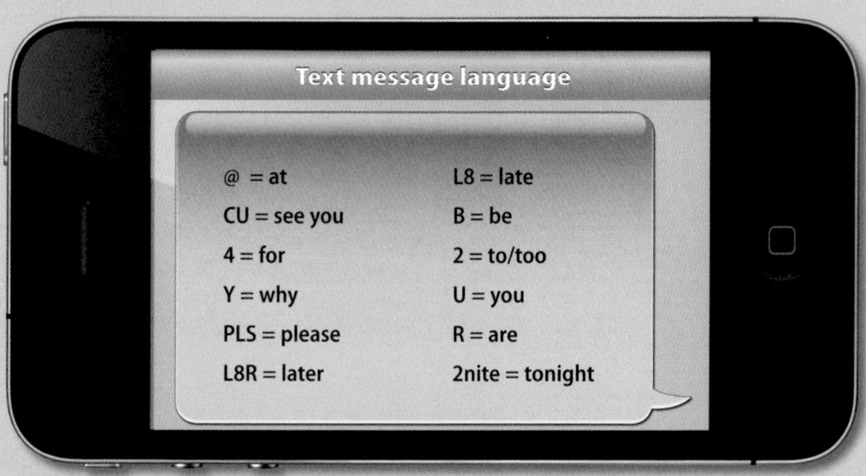

Text message language
@ = at
CU = see you
4 = for
Y = why
PLS = please
L8R = later
L8 = late
B = be
2 = to/too
U = you
R = are
2nite = tonight

1 Look at the messages from and to Emma. Use the key. Write the messages in full.

a From Emma

Al, U R always L8! Fast Cars is looking 4 a new guitar player. PLS don't worry about us. We don't need U any more. GOODBYE!

Al, you are always late! *Fast Cars*

....

....

....

b To Emma

Y RU doing this? PLS don't B angry. We need 2 talk. RU @ home L8R? Al

Why ....?

....

....

....

2 Complete the text message exchanges. Choose from the abbreviations in the box.

a From Jack

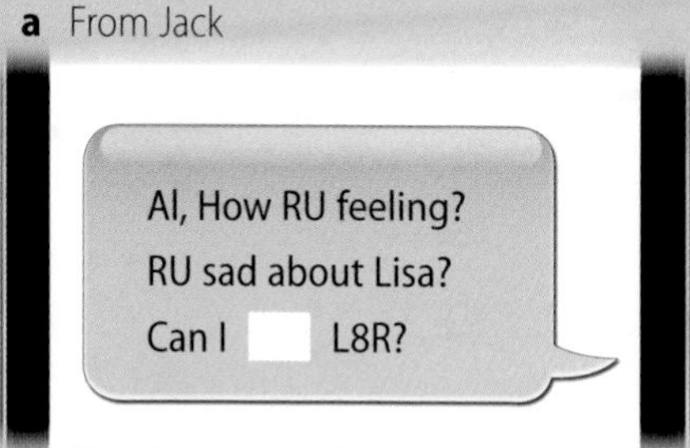

To Jack

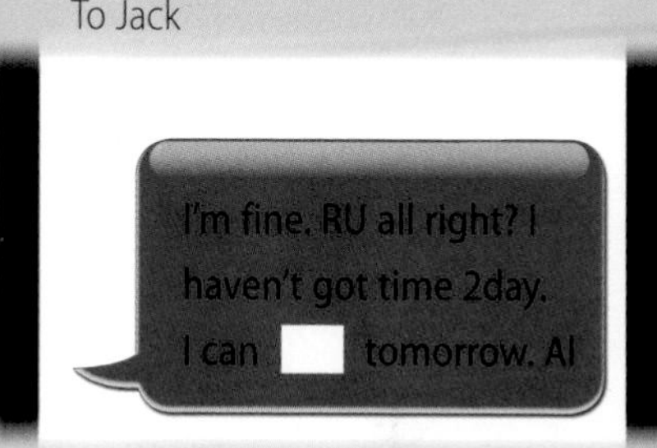

b From Ben

To Ben

c From Emma

To Emma

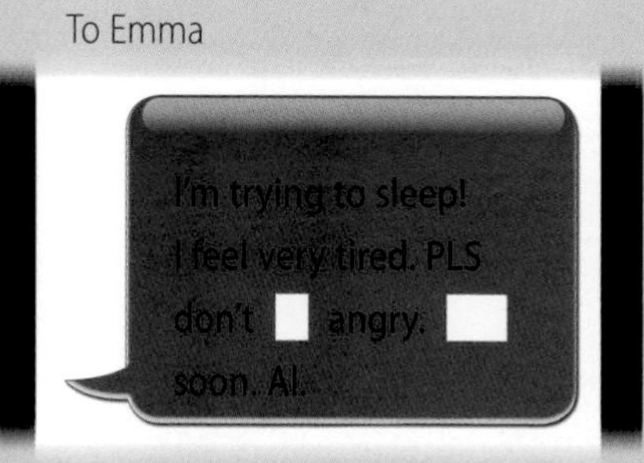

3 Write a text message from one person in the story to a different person.

4 Give your message to a partner. First they must answer these questions about it.

a Who in the story is it from?

b Who in the story is it to?

c What is it about?

Then they must write an answering message.

WORD WORK 1

1 Match the words from Chapter 1 and the pictures.

a parent

b drums

c music

d band

e baby

f guitar

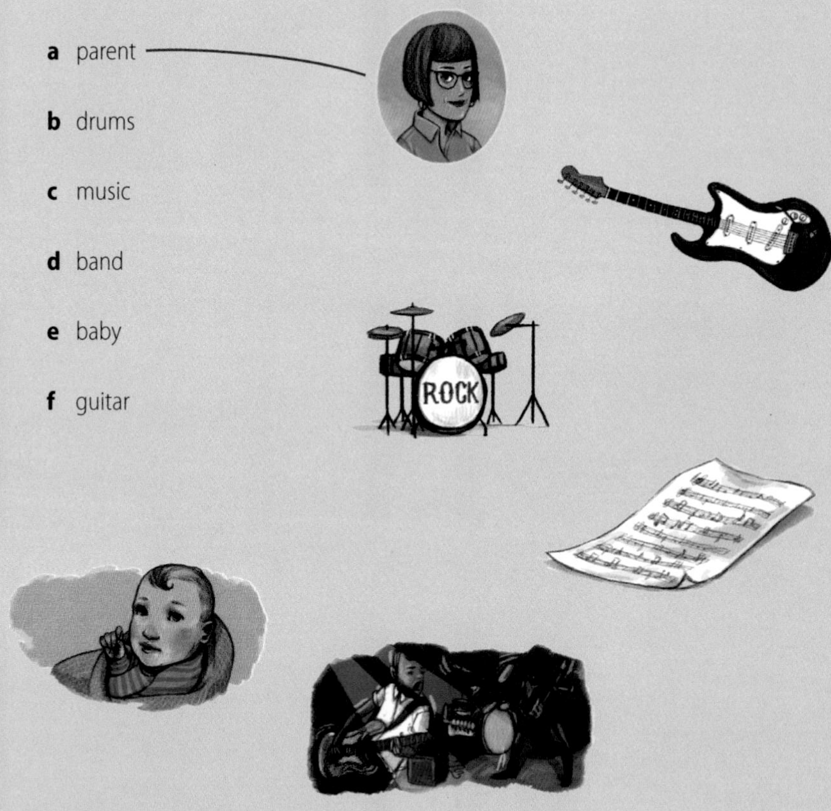

2 Complete each sentence with the best word from Chapter 2.

alone	short	homework	concentrate	try	~~hospital~~

a Lisa must go to ...hospital... because she is ill.

b His hair isn't long. It's ....

c This song isn't easy, but please .... to sing it.

d Jack lives ...., not with his family.

e Al cannot .... because he is tired.

f Can you help me with my Maths .... ?

WORD WORK 2

1 Unscramble the letters and find the words from Chapter 3.

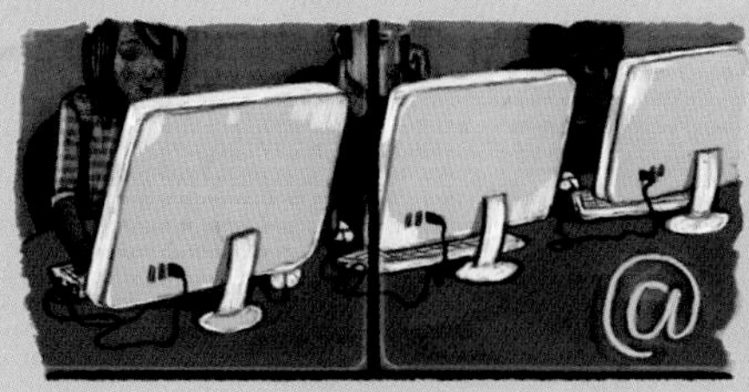

RENTTINE FACÉ

a internet café

YROWR

b _ _ _ _ _

IBOMEL HENOP

c _ _ _ _ _ _ _ _ _ _ _

GRIN

d _ _ _ _

2 Read the clues and complete the puzzle with words from Chapter 4.

a Not easy

b Not happy

c Al can always .... Jack.

d Lisa's .... isn't right.

e You can write this to someone.

f Lisa needs this.

d	i	f	f	i	c	u	l	t
		☐	■	☐				
			■	☐	☐	☐	☐	
			■	☐	☐	☐	☐	
		☐	■	☐	☐	☐	☐	☐
☐	☐	☐	■	☐	☐	☐	☐	☐

What is the word in the dark squares?

Clue: Jack is this. Mr Brown is one of these, too. A _ _ _ _ _ _

WORD WORK 3

1 These words from Chapter 5 don't match the pictures. Correct them.

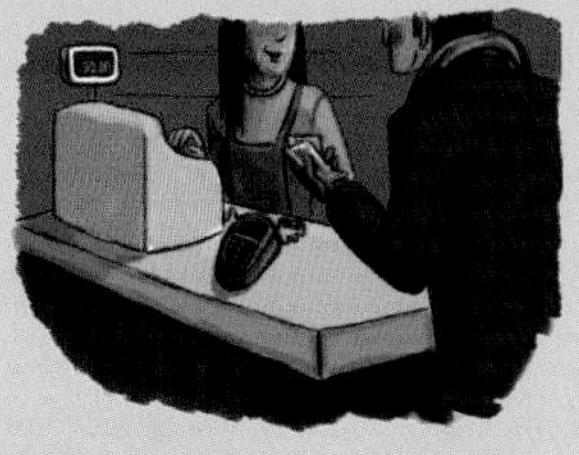

a ~~record~~

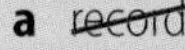

b radio

....

c gig

....

d pay

....

e website

....

f bright

....

2 Complete the sentences with the words from Chapter 6 in the house.

download ~~war~~ bomb drop dance concert experience

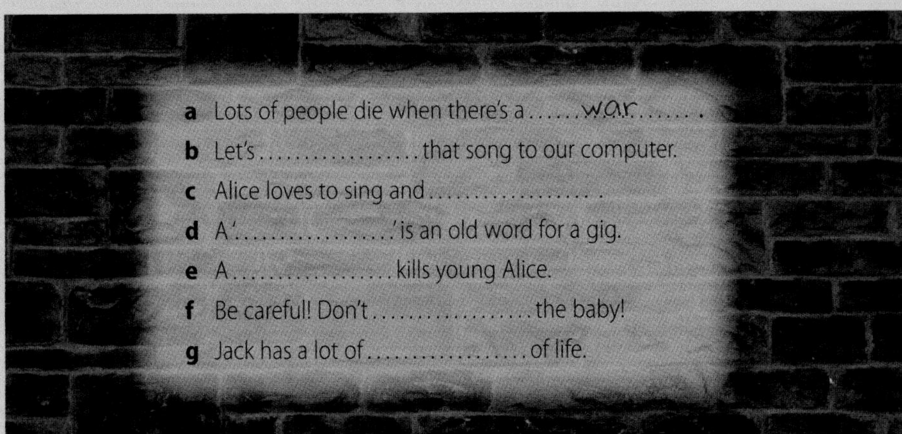

a Lots of people die when there's a ......war...... .

b Let's .... that song to our computer.

c Alice loves to sing and ....

d A '..................' is an old word for a gig.

e A .... kills young Alice.

f Be careful! Don't .... the baby!

g Jack has a lot of .... of life.

GRAMMAR CHECK

Information questions and question words

We use question words in information questions. We answer these questions by giving some information.

Where does Al live?	*In Nottingham.*
Why must Lisa have an operation?	*Because she's very ill.*
How much money do the Browns need?	*A lot.*

1 Complete the information questions with the question words in the box

~~How many~~ What How much Why When Where Which Who

a Q: How many people are there in *Fast Cars*?
A: There are four.

b Q: .... is Emma angry with Al?
A: Because he doesn't listen to her.

c Q: .... is Jack's sister?
A: Alice.

d Q: .... is the name of Al's band?
A: *Fast Cars.*

e Q: .... country can Lisa visit for help?
A: The United States of America.

f Q: .... money have the Browns got?
A: Not much.

g Q: .... does the band meet?
A: At Ben's house.

h Q: .... does Al write *Lisa's Song*?
A: After his talk with Jack.

GRAMMAR CHECK

Present Simple: *Yes/No* questions and short answers

We use auxiliary verbs and be (main verb) in *Yes/No* questions.

In the short answer we reuse the auxiliary verb or be (main verb).

Do you like music?	*Yes, I do.*
Are the Browns American?	*No, they aren't (are not).*

2 Write answers for the questions about the people in the story. Use the short answers in the box.

~~Yes, he does.~~	No, he doesn't.	Yes, they are.	Yes, he does.	Yes, he has.
Yes, she can.	Yes, they do.	No, it isn't.	Yes, he can.	No, she doesn't.

a Does Al live in England? ....Yes, he does....

b Can he play the guitar? ....

c Does he live with Jack? ....

d Has Al got a sister? ....

e Does Al go to school? ....

f Are Emma and Ben in the band? ....

g Does Lisa go to school? ....

h Is life easy for the Browns? ....

i Can Emma sing? ....

j Do Mr and Mrs Brown love their children? ....

3 Write short answers for these questions.

a Is Alice dead? ......Yes, she is.....

b Is Jack happy about that? ....

c Does he think of Alice a lot? ....

d Does Alice leave phone messages for him? ....

e Can Jack change past things? ....

f Can Al and Lisa help him to forget Alice? ....

GRAMMAR CHECK

Linkers: *and, but, so,* and *because*

and links two parts of a sentence with the same idea.

Al can sing and he can write songs, too.

but links two parts of a sentence with different ideas.

Emma can sing but she can't play the guitar.

so links two parts of a sentence talking about the result of something.

Al needs more money so <u>he puts</u> Lisa's Song <u>on the website</u>.

(result of first part of sentence)

because links two parts of a sentence talking about the reason for something.

Lisa stays in hospital because <u>she is very little</u>.

(reason for first part of sentence)

4 Complete the sentences with *and, but, so* or *because*.

a Every day, Al goes to school ......and...... in the evening he plays with the band.
b Lisa is beautiful .... she isn't very well.
c Al visits his grandfather .... he isn't happy at home.
d Lisa needs an operation .... Al must do something.
e Al wants to do his homework .... he is very tired.
f *Fast Cars* want to help Lisa .... they have a gig for her.
g Lisa goes to America .... her parents go with her.
h Al is happy .... he can help his sister.
i Jack can't help Alice .... he can help his grandchildren.
j Jack and Al go the airport .... they don't go to America.

DOMINOES THE STRUCTURED APPROACH TO READING IN ENGLISH

Dominoes is an enjoyable series of illustrated classic and modern stories in four carefully graded language stages – from Starter to Three – which take learners from beginner to intermediate level.

Each *Domino* reader includes:

- a good story to read and enjoy
- integrated activities to develop reading skills and increase active vocabulary
- personalized projects to make the language and story themes more meaningful
- contextualized grammar practice.

Each *Domino* pack contains a reader, plus a MultiROM with:

- a complete audio recording of the story, fully dramatized to bring it to life
- interactive activities to offer further practice in reading and language skills and to consolidate learning.

If you liked this Quick Starter Level *Domino*, why not read these?

The Skateboarder

Christine Lindop

'I love Owen's skateboarding,' Hannah thinks. 'I want to jump and do tricks, too.'

When a skatepark opens near her house, Hannah is suddenly very interested in skateboarding. How do Mom, Dad, brother Evan, and cousin Justin feel about this? Who helps her? Who laughs at her? And who teaches her to be a real skateboarder in the end? This story has the answers.

Book ISBN: 978 0 19 424946 1
MultiROM Pack ISBN: 978 0 19 424944 7

Pebbles on the Beach

Alex Raynham

Abby is a teenager, and doesn't talk much to her parents. Abby's dad works hard for an oil company, and Abby's mom doesn't like her friends. Then, one summer, Abby stays with her crazy Aunt May in California. Here – with Aunt May and her young neighbours Diego and Bianca – she learns to see things differently. But, one night, there's an oil spill on the beautiful beach near their home.

What can Abby, her aunt, and the neighbours do? And who answers Abby's call for more help? And how?

Book ISBN: 978 0 19 424948 5
MultiROM Pack ISBN: 978 0 19 424947 8

You can find details and a full list of books in the Oxford Graded Readers catalogue and Oxford English Language Teaching Catalogue, and on the website: www.oup.com/elt

Teachers: see www.oup.com/elt for a full range of online support, or consult your local office.

	CEF	Cambridge Exams	IELTS	TOEFL iBT	TOEIC
Level 3	B1	PET	4.0	57-86	550
Level 2	A2–B1	KET-PET	3.0-4.0	–	–
Level 1	A1–A2	YLE Flyers/KET	3.0	–	–
Starter	A1	YLE Movers	–	–	–